About Insects

A Guide for Children

Cathryn Sill

Illustrated by John Sill

PEACHTREE
ATLANTA

For the One who created insects.

—Genesis 1:25

Published by
PEACHTREE PUBLISHERS
1700 Chattahoochee Avenue
Atlanta, Georgia 30318-2112
www.peachtree-online.com

Text © 2000, 2015 Cathryn P. Sill
Jacket and interior illustrations © 2000, 2015 John C. Sill

Illustrations created in watercolor on archival quality
100 percent rag watercolor paper
Text and titles set in Novarese from Adobe

Printed in April 2015 by Imago in China

Revised edition
10 9 8 7 6 5 4 3 2 1 (hardcover edition)
10 9 8 7 6 5 4 3 2 1 (trade paperback edition)

Library of Congress Cataloging-in-Publication Data

Sill, Cathryn P., 1953–
　　About insects: a guide for children / Cathryn Sill; illustrated by John Sill.
　　　　p. cm.
　　Summary: Describes the anatomy, behavior, and habitat of various
　　insects, including the beetle, moth, and cockroach.
　　ISBN: 978-1-56145-881-3 (hardcover)
　　ISBN: 978-1-56145-882-0 (trade paperback)
　　1. Insects—Juvenile literature. [1. Insects.] I. Sill, John, ill. II. Title.

　　QL467.2 .S538 2000
　　595.7—dc21

　　　　　　　　　　　　　　99-045785

About Insects

Insects have six legs...

and three body parts.

PLATE 2
Eastern Velvet Ant

They have a waterproof skeleton on the outside of their bodies.

PLATE 3
Giant Stag Beetle

Young insects hatch from eggs.

They go through several changes as they grow up.

PLATE 5
Monarch Butterfly

Antennae help insects smell, taste, and feel.

Some insects suck animals or plants to get food.

Others bite and chew their meals.

PLATE 8
Southeastern Lubber Grasshopper

Many insects fly.

Some crawl because they have no wings.

Others jump...

or swim.

Some are active during the day.

Some insects may be pests.

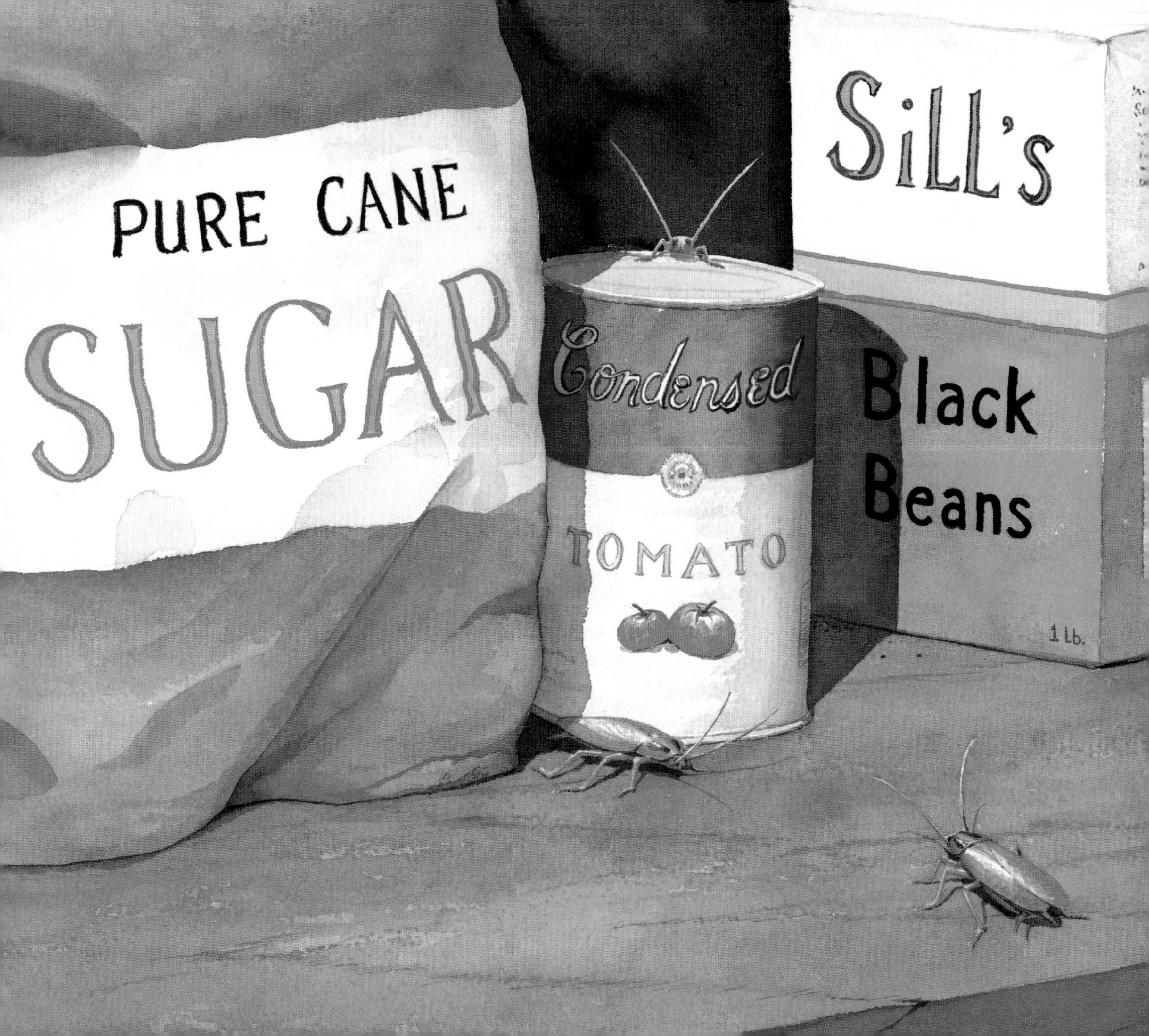
PURE CANE
SUGAR
Condensed
TOMATO
SiLL's
Black
Beans
1 Lb.

But many are very helpful.

Insects are an important part of our world.

Afterword

PLATE 1

Insects are found almost everywhere and are the most numerous of all animals. Over 1 million species have been identified. Some experts believe there are 2 million to 30 million insects that have never been discovered and named. Dogbane Leaf Beetles live throughout the eastern United States and southern Canada. They leak a bad-smelling liquid to stay safe from predators.

PLATE 2

The three parts of an insect's body are the head, the thorax, and the abdomen. The antennae, eyes, and mouth are located on the head. The legs and wings are attached to the thorax. Organs in the abdomen allow insects to digest food, breathe, and reproduce. Eastern Velvet Ants are antlike wasps with such a painful sting that they are sometimes called "cow killers." They live in the eastern United States.

PLATE 3

Insects have hard coverings called exoskeletons. "Exo" means "outside." The insect's muscles are attached to the inside of the exoskeleton. Stag beetles get their name from their huge jaws, which look like the antlers of a stag. Males use their jaws for fighting each other. There are about 1,200 species of stag beetles around the world. Giant Stag Beetles live around rotting oak stumps in the eastern United States and west to Oklahoma.

PLATE 4

Insects grow up by a process called "metamorphosis." Some insects go through simple metamorphosis with three stages of growth—egg, nymph, and adult. The female Praying Mantis squeezes a special foam from her body and lays 100 to 200 eggs in the foam. It hardens and protects the eggs until they are ready to hatch. Each egg hatches into a nymph that looks like a tiny version of the adult. Praying Mantises are native to southern Europe. They were first brought to North America in 1889 on a shipment of plants.

PLATE 5

Butterflies and many other insects develop by complete metamorphosis. They go through four stages of development—egg, larva, pupa, and adult. An adult lays an egg that produces a wormlike larva. The larva feeds and grows, then changes into a pupa. When the pupa is fully developed, an adult insect emerges. Monarch Butterflies are the only butterflies that have a two-way migration. They live in most of North America.

PLATE 6

Antennae, which are found on the front of an insect's head, are sometimes called "feelers." They are sense organs that help insects find food and locate enemies. The shape and size of antennae varies for different kinds of insects. Virginia Ctenuchid Moths have feathery antennae. They live in southern Canada and the northern United States.

PLATE 7

Most flies have mouthparts that lap up liquids. Horse fly females suck blood from mammals after slicing the skin with scissor-like mouthparts. Males drink nectar from flowers. There are many kinds of horse flies around the world. Black Horse Flies are common in the eastern United States.

PLATE 8

Insects such as grasshoppers bite and chew their food by moving their mandibles (jaws) from side to side. Grasshoppers live in grasslands, fields, meadows, and forests all over the world. Southeastern Lubber Grasshoppers live on roadsides, in field edges, and in gardens in the southeastern United States.

PLATE 9

Most adult insects have two pairs of wings attached to the thorax. Some insects have only one pair of wings. Dragonflies have four wings that move independently, enabling them to fly backward as well as forward. Common Whitetails catch and eat small insects while in flight. They are found through most of the United States and southern Canada.

PLATE 10

Some insects mimic parts of the plants on which they live. Giant Walkingsticks look so much like twigs that predators easily overlook them. Measuring nearly six inches (150 cm), they are the longest insects in North America. Giant Walkingsticks live in the southeastern and midwestern United States.

PLATE 11

Strong muscles in their back legs help some insects jump long distances. Many insects that jump make sounds by rubbing one body part against another. Katydids and crickets "sing" by raising their wings and rubbing them together. Gladiator Meadow Katydids live in the northern half of the United States and in southern Canada.

PLATE 12

Beetles that live in lakes, ponds, rivers, and streams have paddle-shaped back legs that help them swim. Whirligig Beetles swim around on the surface of the water. They can also fly and dive underwater. Whirligig Beetles' eyes are divided into two parts so they are able to see above and below the surface of the water. There are around 700 species of Whirligig Beetles around the world. They live throughout North America.

PLATE 13

Insects are found in almost every habitat on the earth, but very few of them are able to live in the salty water in oceans. Silverfish are found all over the world in warm, moist places. Outdoors they live under fallen leaves, rocks, and logs. Indoors they are found in attics, basements, behind furniture, and near sinks or bathtubs. They eat many things, including plants, clothing, dry foods, paper, and bookbindings.

PLATE 14

Animals that are active in the daytime are called "diurnal." Honeybees live in colonies or large groups that work together. The worker bees spend warm days gathering food from flowers. They eat pollen and nectar. Honeybees use nectar to make honey to eat in winter when flowers are not blooming. Settlers brought honeybees to North America from Europe during the 1600s.

PLATE 15

Most moths are nocturnal (active at night). Luna Moth caterpillars eat tree leaves. Adults do not eat at all. They reproduce and then die. Luna Moths were once common but are now rare because of insecticides and pollutants. They live in North America east of the Great Plains.

PLATE 16

Insects are considered pests when they annoy or harm people. Some insects can destroy valuable crops, have irritating bites or stings, carry disease, infest food supplies, or damage wooden buildings. German Cockroaches have an unpleasant odor and search for food in homes, restaurants, and food factories. They live all over the world wherever people live.

PLATE 17

Many insects help humans by eating other insects that destroy crops. Lady beetle (also called "ladybug") larvae and adults eat aphids and other small insects. Farmers and gardeners often buy lady beetles and turn them loose near crops that are harmed by aphids. Convergent Lady Beetles are common throughout North America and parts of South America.

PLATE 18

Insects are an important food source for animals. They pollinate many of the plants that provide food for us. Insects produce useful products such as honey, beeswax, and silk. Some people enjoy watching insects and learning about their habits. Mayfly nymphs live in clean fresh water. As they become adults, they leave the water and grow wings. There are thousands of kinds of mayflies around the world and hundreds in North America.

GLOSSARY

habitat—the place where animals and plants live

insecticide—a chemical used to kill insects

organ—a part of an animal's body that does a specific job (for example, eyes, lungs, heart)

pollutant—anything that makes water, air, or land unclean or impure

predator—an animal that lives by hunting and eating other animals

reproduce—to have babies

species—a group of animals or plants that are alike in many ways

true bug—an insect with sucking, beaklike mouthparts

two-way migration—the movement of an animal from its birthplace to a warmer place for winter and then back in summer.

SUGGESTIONS FOR FURTHER READING

BOOKS

INSECTS: (GOLDEN GUIDE) by Clarence Cottam and Herbert Zim (St. Martin's Press)

KAUFMAN FIELD GUIDE TO INSECTS OF NORTH AMERICA by Eric R. Eaton and Kenn Kaufman (Houghton Mifflin)

PETERSON FIRST GUIDE TO INSECTS OF NORTH AMERICA by Christopher Leahy (Houghton Mifflin)

WEBSITES

www.insectidentification.org
www.biokids.umich.edu/critters/Insecta
www.bugfacts.net/index.php#.U4TiBCibLVo

ABOUT... SERIES

ISBN 978-1-56145-234-7 HC
ISBN 978-1-56145-312-2 PB

ISBN 978-1-56145-038-1 HC
ISBN 978-1-56145-364-1 PB

ISBN 978-1-56145-688-8 HC
ISBN 978-1-56145-699-4 PB

ISBN 978-1-56145-301-6 HC
ISBN 978-1-56145-405-1 PB

ISBN 978-1-56145-256-9 HC
ISBN 978-1-56145-335-1 PB

ISBN 978-1-56145-588-1 HC
ISBN 978-1-56145-837-0 PB

ISBN 978-1-56145-881-3 HC
ISBN 978-1-56145-882-0 PB

ISBN 978-1-56145-757-1 HC
ISBN 978-1-56145-758-8 PB

ISBN 978-1-56145-358-0 HC
ISBN 978-1-56145-407-5 PB

ISBN 978-1-56145-331-3 HC
ISBN 978-1-56145-406-8 PB

ISBN 978-1-56145-795-3 HC

ISBN 978-1-56145-743-4 HC
ISBN 978-1-56145-741-0 PB

ISBN 978-1-56145-536-2 HC
ISBN 978-1-56145-811-0 PB

ISBN 978-1-56145-183-8 HC
ISBN 978-1-56145-233-0 PB

ISBN 978-1-56145-454-9 HC

ALSO AVAILABLE
IN BILINGUAL EDITION

- About Birds / Sobre los pájaros
  ISBN 978-1-56145-783-0 PB
- About Mammals / Sobre los mamíferos
  ISBN 978-1-56145-800-4 PB
- About Insects / Sobre los insectos
  ISBN 978-1-56145-883-7 PB

ABOUT HABITATS SERIES

ISBN 978-1-56145-641-3 HC
ISBN 978-1-56145-636-9 PB

ISBN 978-1-56145-734-2 HC

ISBN 978-1-56145-559-1 HC

ISBN 978-1-56145-469-3 HC
ISBN 978-1-56145-731-1 PB

ISBN 978-1-56145-618-5 HC

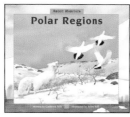

ISBN 978-1-56145-832-5 HC

ISBN 978-1-56145-432-7 HC
ISBN 978-1-56145-689-5 PB

THE SILLS

CATHRYN AND JOHN SILL are the dynamic team who created the *About…* series as well as the *About Habitats* series. Their books have garnered praise from educators and have won a variety of awards, including Bank Street Best Books, CCBC Choices, NSTA/CBC Outstanding Science Trade Books for Students K–12, Orbis Pictus Recommended, and *Science Books and Films* Best Books of the Year. Cathryn, a graduate of Western Carolina State University, taught early elementary school classes for thirty years. John holds a BS in wildlife biology from North Carolina State University. Combining his artistic skill and knowledge of wildlife, he has achieved an impressive reputation as a wildlife artist. The Sills live in Franklin, North Carolina.